Overcoming Your Self-Schema

How to Wipe Away Your Faults

By H.T. Stewart

Published by Make Profits Easy LLC

Profitsdaily123@aol.com

facebook.com/MakeProfitsEasy

Table of Contents

Introduction..5

Chapter One: What Is Self-Schema? 7

Chapter Two: Self-Schema's Missing Parts....... 13

Chapter Three: How Your Self-Schema Is Created.. 16

Who Influences Your Self-Schema 18

How Social Status Influences Self-Schema ... 19

How Sexual Influences Can Shape A Self-Schema 22

Men's Sexual Self-Schemas 24

Women's Sexual Self-Schemas 26

Creating Our Concept of 'Self' 28

Chapter Four: Why You Have Multiple Self-Schemas.. 31

Chapter Five: Negative Self-Schemas Effects On Your Body.. 34

Our Body Self-Schema.................................... 35

Negative Self-Schemas That Shame Your 'Self' 37

Chapter Six: How To Gain Control Of Your Self-Schema.. 44

Chapter Seven: Making Positive Changes To Your Self-Schema 85

Chapter Eight: Creating The Self-Schema You Want.. 96

Conclusion.. 108

Introduction

Our personal body image and how we view our own personalities has a profound effect on everything in our lives from the car we choose to our jobs to who we choose for romantic relationships. Multiple factors go into creating our self-image and how we identify ourselves, which is also called our self-schema. For many people, their self-schema lands in the middle, not too positive but not too negative either.

However, there are some people out there – you perhaps – who have let their self-schema rule their lives for too long. You want to change for the better, you want to have that outgoing personality that you've always dreamed of, and you want to have a better outlook for your life in general.

That is why you are here – to learn how to reprogram your self-schema and create the personality traits that you want to have.

In this book, we will go through what the self-schema is, how it is formed, what it controls, and how you can change it for the better. We will take you through the whole process so that you can begin to transform your self-schema into one that helps you land that new job, find the perfect soul mate, and be a better rounded person.

Chapter One: What Is Self-Schema?

In the realm of psychology, there is a huge question that deals with our self-schemas and our body: is the self a subset of the body or is the body a subset of the self? Is our mind just as simplified as our brain being set in our skull, with our conscious being an after effect of that pairing? Or is our body simply a creation of the mind, something we do not actually have control over, except for our own perceptions about the sensations we have? Psychologists have mulled over this question, and the implications of both answers, for a long time with no unified answer.

It is this nagging question that brings us to our multiple layers of self-schema and how they create automated responses from our mind and body to different situations and stimuli. It is also this question that brings us to discuss the 'conceptual' experience of our own bodies, such as what we are told through science, old wives' tales, myths, etc. These experiences and what we learn about our body then creates our beliefs about ourselves.

If you have not heard the term 'self-schema' before, then chances are that you are not aware that this is something everyone has ingrained in them already. Self-schema is a stable, long term set of memories that make up your personal belief system. This system includes everything that you currently believe and think about your experiences, yourself as a person and yourself as an emotional being. Your beliefs based on yourself as a person can include any of your physical characteristics, your personality, your interests, your job, and so on – anything that you deem important to your own self-definition of who you are.

Here is an example of a self-schema that many people have who are, or consider themselves to be, extroverted. Extroverted people think of themselves as extroverts, they also believe that this is a central pillar of their lives. When asked about categorizing their personality with a set of statements, they will often check that they are sociable people, that they have many friends, that they speak to a lot of people they do not know, and other statements that show they are outgoing. Introverted people will have the opposite markers on their statements, because they believe that they are introverted people.

Self-schema is basically a schematic for your life and yourself as a whole. Those who are professional politicians will have a schema for that dimension of their lives as someone who makes decisions, who is outgoing, and who can impact people's lives. Those who are pop stars will have a schema for a public performing figure who can perform in front of large crowds, who has an over the top personality, and who can influence their audience.

Your self-schema will have a variety of different factors that contribute to the whole of who you are. These stem from your cultural beliefs and how you grew up. If you grew up in the United States, your beliefs and views will be different than someone who grew up in South Korea or Egypt. Also, if you grew up in the Southern United States, your beliefs will be different than those from the Northern United States. These beliefs will also vary depending on your religious affiliation, your family views, and where you live.

Once you've developed your self-schema, it tends to rule your life in what you do, what jobs you choose, who you become involved with romantically, who your friends are, and every aspect of your life. This self-schema is your personal bias to your own beliefs about yourself. As you grow, few things can change or alter your self-schema. Even as an adult, you may not even realize that your self-schema controls everything you say and do and very little can change it until you understand that it is in control.

As you grow into an adult, your self-schema is firmly set and stored in your long term memory. The area of your brain that stores your long term memory is also the area that controls the information that is processed for your personality and yourself as a whole. For example, if you develop a self-schema that hates to work out, you're not going to work out or even enjoy it as much as someone who's self-schema loves to work out.

Now that you know a little about what self-schemas are, let's talk about pieces of our schemas that are missing and why it is ok to having missing parts.

Chapter Two: Self-Schema's Missing Parts

There will always be parts of any self-schema that are missing. These parts are called achematic and it just means that you do not have a schematic for a particular area of your personality. This usually happens when someone does not have to worry about a certain attribute of themselves. For example, if you go to school and train to be an artist, chances are that you are not concerned with being a veterinarian or a corporate accountant. Therefore, those parts of your self-schema do not have any set rules and will be missing.

You will have missing parts for other aspects of your life as well. If you are raised in a Catholic church, you will not have any type of schema for being a Buddhist. However, just because you are missing a part does not mean that you are biased against the part you do not have. Instead, it means that you have no bias deep down and it has to be learned through the culture that you have grown up in.

The good news is that these types of missing self-schemas are one of the easiest to replace because there was nothing there to begin with. For areas that do not have an imprinted self-schema, you can easily begin to practice what you would like to put in that area now. For example, if you have no opinion or dealing with someone in another country and you find yourself working with a new coworker from that country, it will be easy to learn about their country without any reservations. You will be able to form a new self-schema about that country, and that new coworker, without any hesitate from your inner psyche.

Chapter Three: How Your Self-Schema Is Created

Now that we have talked about what a self-schema is and how you can have missing parts, it is time to discuss how they are created. Just like your personality, your face, and your fingerprints, there are no two self-schemas that are alike. Every person has a different self-schema because their lives and experiences are different. Even twins will have different self-schemas because they do not share the exact same experiences that the other does. They might be extremely close, but never the same.

We are all exposed to the idea of 'self' from an early age. This exposure comes from parents, siblings, close family and friends, and other figures that are prominent in our childhoods. At first, the self-schema that we take on is very basic and involves either being a 'good' or 'bad' child. Everything is broken down into these positive or negative terms and is pretty easy to understand. Gradually, as you grow, you begin to try to explain your action or you are asked to explain them. So, the concept of a positive/negative view of 'self' becomes more complicated.

Almost every schema that makes up a person's view of their 'self' has bipolar aspects. These are aspects like healthy versus sick, quiet versus loud, inactive versus active, and so on. While these aspects are usually considered as traits too, when it comes to self-schemas, everyone has a middle ground that they stand on between two opposing aspects.

Let's take a closer look at what forms the different parts of your main self-schemas.

Who Influences Your Self-Schema

As you grow up, the people who influence your life will have an impact on your self-schema. If you grow up with parents who always want to stay in the house and watch tv, then you can have two severely different outcomes for your self-schema. You will either have that imprinted on your own views or you will want to be the opposite of that and be a very active person. If your parents or guardians were extremely dishonest, you will either follow in those footsteps or you will strive to be an honest person.

Generally, you are going to follow in the footsteps of those that have the most influence on your personality. If you have a parent or grandparent that you are very close to who is extremely honest and trustworthy, chances are that will be imprinted on your self-schema. However, your self-schema is programmed as you grow up, that is how it will continue to grow as you get older.

How Social Status Influences Self-Schema

On top of this, every person will have their own different set of social and life experiences that will alter and imprint their self-schema. Some of the different labels that can imprint on your self-schema as you grow up include: lazy, geek, loud, outgoing, shy, jock, nerd, funny, dumb, smart, or quiet. Depending on how you begin to be labeled by peers in school and social situations, those labels will begin to imprint on your self-schema and form how you see yourself.

If you were a football player all through grade school and high school, chances are that you have the self-schema of an athlete or 'jock'. You see yourself as someone who likes to perform in front of people on the field. You are able to focus on exercise and physical exertion to make correct plays. You have the ability to be outgoing on the field around new teams and players. So, in your everyday life, those pieces of your athletic self-schema will spill over. Chances are that you're going to be more outgoing.

On the other hand, if you have always thought of yourself as a 'nerd' or 'geek', then you're going to automatically gravitate toward activities that feed that persona. You may take more classes and be part of groups that are involved in computer programming, creating video games, writing blogs about cult TV shows or movies, etc. Chances are that you're going to be a bit more shy because most self-schemas that revolve around these types of personas are more introverted.

How Sexual Influences Can Shape A Self-Schema

As the world around us develops, so do our perceptions of what is considered sexy and the emphasis that society puts on sex. Psychologists know that sex has a developmental control over everyone's personalities as we grow. The push to establish intimate relationships throughout our adult lives is taught as we grow up. These relationships, and how we view them, both shapes and controls our self-schemas about relationships, sex, and our own bodies. The psychological school of thought is that depending on how you use your sexuality, your sexual nature will then be centralized in the same way. For example, if you put a high focus and value on your sexual nature, that will become a large part of your self-schema and controlling identity. If you don't focus as much on that aspect, then your controlling self-schema will put other aspects of your personality above your sexual nature.

However, it's not just how your sexual nature controls your identity. If you consider that your self-schemas are like a mental framework that helps to keep outside social stimuli and your reactions to them separate and organized. So, your different views of your 'self' only come out when you are in specific social situations. Your sexual schemas are a generalized view of your sexual aspects of your 'self'. This view comes from previous experiences, social stimuli, movies, books, tv, and everything around you. It then manifests itself in any current experiences that you are involved in, and influences how you process any new socially sexual information and helps guide you in future sexual behavior.

Due to the way that sexual schemas work, men and women will experience their sexual 'self' in different ways. Although they have different experiences, psychologists have found that both sexes believe that a 'sexual person' can have better qualities, such as passion, romance, love, and arousal, and have better intimate relationships.

Men's Sexual Self-Schemas

Men have a wide spectrum for their sexual schemas that runs from being very schematic to chaotic. Men with a schematic view of their sexual schema will be more aggressive, open minded, powerful, and liberal in their attitudes about sex. They will also be more experienced as they tend to have a higher number of sexual relationships, usually without any type of commitment. However, they consider being single as just a temporary situation. These men will also be more likely to fall in love as they have a high capacity for romance, passion, and love.

On the other side of the spectrum, men who have a chaotic view of sexual schemas, or aschematic, have a bit of a harder time with sexual relationships. Men with this side of the sexual self-schema will have a smaller range of sexual relationships and are normally single the majority of the time. Because they are single, they fall into a pattern of talking themselves out of relationships and pushing potential sexual partners or intimate relationships away. Their self-schemas are then caught in a circle where they believe that they will be single forever.

Women's Sexual Self-Schemas

Women have different sexual self-schemas that are composed of three different things, two of them positive and one of them negative. The positive aspects are a passionate-romantic aspect and an open-direct view of themselves. The negative aspect is a conservative view of themselves that can lead to embarrassment.

Due to these three aspects, women who have stronger positive aspects are able to dominate that negative one and overcome it in their lives.

Positive sexual schemas for women will give them a more open view when it comes to being emotionally and romantically open for a new relationship and experiences that come along with it. They also will be more liberal in their attitudes about sex, meaning that they will be able to overcome social hurdles that other women will face. These women are also able to evaluate behaviors associated with sexual schemas in a positive light which does lead to more uncommitted sexual encounters, such as one-night stands, and anticipate more partners in the future. But this positive view of sexual behaviors will also allow these types of women to have more romantic partners as well as put a higher value on relationships and loving attachments.

For women with a negative view of their sexual self-schema, they tend to consider themselves as a 'cold' person, someone who doesn't like or value romance, and someone who is not open to sexual relationships very often. Women who allow a negative view to overtake their sexual schemas will find that they are not confident when it comes to sexual topics in social situations or intimate relationships. They are more likely to be single and stay single.

Creating Our Concept of 'Self'

Since we are told from birth about ourselves from our parents and others, our concepts about our 'self' begins to create itself almost immediately. As we start to interact with other people, we begin to develop other views of the 'self' in social relationships and situations. We start to meet more new people as we grow and go to school, we join new groups and make new friends, which constantly update our view of the 'self'. This is also how we begin to develop self-schemas and then multiple schemas.

Every one of our different schemas merge together and create our 'self-concept'. These self-concepts are extremely complex as they are made of all of our schemas (both positive and negative), merging everything we have known, changed, and learned into one large view. Our self-concept is always changing and updating as we learn new things, meet new people, and go throughout our lives.

Your self-schemas will always continue to change and adapt to situations around you. Due to this constant state of change, your view of your 'self' will be in an ever fluid state as well. It is for this reason that you can overcome the negative self-schemas that you have developed in your life and change them into the positive ones that you want to have.

Chapter Four: Why You Have Multiple Self-Schemas

Now that you know how self-schemas are created, let's take a look at the multiple schemas that your psyche creates. As you continue to grow, you will subconsciously create multiple self-schemas that will control how you function in different areas of your life. Believe it or not, but having multiple self-schemas are healthy and can be extremely helpful.

Almost every person alive has at least two sets of schematics for themselves, or two self-schemas. If you have two jobs, if you juggle family and a job, or if you have a hobby that is different than your job, chances are that you have two as well. You may be a salesperson during the day but sing karaoke three nights a week. You may be an executive and a mother. You may be an artist and a computer programmer. No matter who you are, you have set rules that your self-schema puts in place on who you are. We will discuss multiple self-schemas in a later chapter.

These different interacting schemas are created as you have different experiences and take on different roles in your life. For example, you will develop a schema when you get married, when you become a parent, when you start college, when you start down a new career path, if you start to play a sport, etc. Every different aspect of your life can develop its own schema and those multiple self-schemas will entwine, giving you the ability to slide seamlessly from one role into another.

Multiple self-schemas will allow your subconscious mind to make fast decisions and have the correct behavior in different situations or around different groups of people. They all work together to take in information and interpret the information in a useful fashion as you navigate different aspects of your life. These different schemas will also program verbal, cognitive, and behavioral actions that will help you perform or act correctly in any situation. In cognitive psychology, these actions are called action plans or scripts.

Each one of your multiple self-schemas vary by the circumstances that you are in, who you are with, your environment, and even your mood.

Chapter Five: Negative Self-Schemas Effects On Your Body

Now that you know how schemas are created and why we have them, let's take a look at how they can affect your body in many different ways. Your mind does more than just keep your heart pumping and your lungs breathing. It keeps the self and the body functioning together in harmony. Your understanding of your own body is vital to creating self-schemas and they make up special schemas, body schemas, that relate just to your body.

Unfortunately, self-schemas go further than simply controlling the classes that we take and how we interact with other people. Self-schema can affect your body and your overall health. If someone considers themselves a 'sick' person, then they may tend to have hypochondriac tendencies, even when they are not really sick. On the flip side, if you consider yourself to be 'healthy', chances are that you're going to be more concerned with exercise, making healthy food choices, and so on.

Our Body Self-Schema

Your body image is created by your self-schemas and becomes its own type of schema as you get older, the body schema. Self-schema that deals with your body will have an influence on what type of foods you buy, how many times a week you exercise, what style of clothing you wear, and the activities that you do with friends. For women, self-schema can have a very problematic effect due to the fact that society places a large focus on how a woman looks and what size she is. This can cause a negative self-schema that will change how a woman takes care of herself, how healthy she is, and can even make some go overboard with exercise, diet, and more.

Everything around us adds to our body self-schema. We are constantly bombarded with views of how the 'perfect' man or woman should look, how they should dress, how their hair should be styled, and so on. These outside views will have an effect on your own body image, no matter how hard you try to ignore them. Even your family and friends will have an influence on your body schema whether they are consciously doing it or not. A simple comment from a friend joking about how your hips look huge in that striped skirt will have an effect on a woman's self-schema no matter what size she is. She can be a size 2 and still have a constant worry that her hips are too big. Knowing this can help you

consciously make efforts to not add negative
views to your own family and friends.

Negative Self-Schemas That Shame Your 'Self'

When you hear the term 'negative', you automatically know it is something bad. However, we still allow negative thoughts and opinions to cloud our own self-schemas. People around us do not always mean to project negative thoughts on us nor do they mean to come out and say something negative. Sometimes, they are just being negative people and intentionally try to put negative issues on another person. We will talk more about overcoming those problems later in our book.

For now, we are going to talk about how negative instructions and information are given to us constantly throughout the day. In social situations, we are given instructions before we have much engagement in a situation. For example, if you are the last person picked for a dodgeball team, the others around you are giving you negative information about how they believe you are not athletic. If you are one of the three people not chosen to serve on a committee at work, the others around you are giving you negative information about how they see your opinion. Even if they did not have that intention, and even if they do not feel that way, your 'self' just took notes that people do not think you are athletic or they do not value your opinions. Of course, the opposite is true as well when it comes to positive instructions, such as being chosen as a team captain for dodgeball.

We take unspoken social instructions constantly from the time we start interacting with other people when we are born. As we grow, our minds learn to automatically gather those instructions and plug them into our self-schemas. You may have the self-schema that you are sloppy because you were always being told to clean your room. You may have a self-schema that you are not artistic or creative because your artwork was never chosen to hang in the principal's office. Or you may have the self-schema that you are not athletic because you were chosen last for every sports team.

Does that mean that your mother, your teacher, or your coach intentionally gave you negative views of yourself? Of course not. But these are real life examples where you can understand how negative instructions are imprinted on your idea of 'self' without there being any malice or intention in them. We simply have learned from a very young age to take the instructions we are given from those around us and put them in our 'self' view.

While psychologists know that this automatic buy in to the negative instructions that we are given happens constantly, they still have yet to understand why. It is this automatic negative buy in coupled with a development of a negative self-schema that we begin to develop shameful feelings about different aspects of our 'self'. Shame is a seriously negative view about some aspect of our 'self' that manifests itself in thousands of different ways. Being anorexic is one way, overachievement is another, and self-destruction is yet another way that shame seeps into our view of our 'self' and begins to physically manifest in hurtful ways. Shame is not a specific condition or emotion that you pinpoint, instead it is considered more of a sensible issue for your self-schemas.

So, how does shame manifest itself in destructive ways? Well, let's take the example of someone who suffers from anorexia. Their body self-schema has been damaged to the point that they actually want to disappear. Negative instructions, intentional or perceived, seep into the view of the 'self' and begin to wear away positive views that are already established.

Over time, that person begins to feel so badly about their body, no matter their size, that they cannot bring themselves to eat. They will actively go out of their way to not eat, and do not see the consequences of their actions until a family member or friend has to intervene. In this case, if there is no intervention in a timely manner, someone can easily allow their personal body shame deteriorate their health to the point that they cannot survive for very long. Even if an intervention does happen quickly, the damage that shame can do physically can cause life-long problems.

Of course, this is not the only example of how shame can cause serious problems by allowing the negative instructions that imprint on our self-schemas to rule our positive ones. Shame is not picky and can easily take the form of any part

of your self-schema and then use that part

against you. The great thing is that shame and

negative instructions can be deprogrammed

from your self-schema. It is something that can

be changed.

Chapter Six: How To Gain Control Of Your Self-Schema

You probably had no idea that negative self-schemas were created so easily that we do not even know they are being implemented. Additionally, you may not have realized that we are bombarded with negativity and instructions from every aspect of our day from the time we are born until we pass on. However, now that you know information is imprinted on you constantly, it will be easier to catch it before it begins to eat away at positive self-schemas that you have built. Believe it or not, but knowing that information of all types is being projected on your self-schema constantly is key to gaining control of it.

Many people that have a negative self-schema that is out of control have signs that they can easily see if they look. These signs are obvious to friends and family, however, you have to stop and take a look at your own self-schema to finally see them for yourself. Since you are reading this book, you already have taken the first step in removing negative information from your self-schema. Here are several signs that you can look at to determine if negative information has made too big of an impact on your self-schemas:

1. You constantly apologize – For example, someone bumps into you when you were standing still and you apologize to them. If you catch yourself wanting to apologize for anything, especially something small,

stop and ask yourself if the apology is actually needed. If someone bumped into you, should you be the one apologizing? No, you should not. Remind yourself that you are not the one who is in the wrong.

2. You always slouch – For example, no matter where you are, you are always humped over. We all slouch every now and then, especially if we are tired. However, people that have let negative information lower their self-schema will tend to slouch constantly. Once you are conscious that you do this, you can take steps to fix it. When you realize that you are slouching, force yourself to sit up straight and fix your posture. You will find

that it not only will help your own self-

schema, but others will notice it too.

3. You only want to lose some pounds for

    aesthetic reasons – For example, you only

    want to drop some weight because you

    think it will help you at work or in your

    social life. If you find that you are putting

    losing weight or changing your body over

    spending time with your family and

    friends – and not for health reasons –

    then your negative self-schema is working

    hard against you. You should only strive

    to lose weight for health reason and for

    your own self, not for any other reason.

4. You compare your body to others – For

    example, you stress over the fact that your

    waist is not as small as Jennifer Lawrence

or your chest is not as big as The Rock. Our society has always put us against each other when it comes to body sizes and looks. When you allow negative self-schemas to get into your 'self', it will skew your view of your own body.

5. You seem to always be telling stupid lies for no reason – For example, you constantly are asking yourself why you said something after it has left your lips. Everyone tells white lies occasionally. However, if you realize that you do it too often or you are always wondering why you just said something, chances are that you are trying to hide your true feelings or thoughts about a subject. Instead, try telling the truth and make a serious effort

to do so. You will find the response will
not be more positive than you imagined.

6. You always back down to make someone
    else happy – For example, you constantly
    back down in conversations when
    someone disagrees with you so you can
    avoid any type of confrontation. To avoid
    conflict at all costs, negative information
    has imprinted on your self-schema that
    you cannot have any type of opposing
    view from anyone. By doing this, you
    never have the chance to have your voice
    heard during conversations. You can use
    positive affirmations daily to help boost
    your self-esteem and create a positive self-
    schema about how you feel.

7. You never leave the house without putting on make-up, fixing your hair, or constantly checking the mirror before you leave – For example, you have to check the mirror by the door twice before you can leave the house to make sure that you look ok. This is an extremely common problem for the majority of the people in the world. For too long people have been imprinted with ideas of what 'beautiful' people should look like. We are told that make up, that stylish haircut, and specific clothing styles are what it takes to be 'cool' and if you do not have them, then you are not good enough. One of the ways that you can work through this is to work on a positive body image and self-schema.

8. You always talk about your 'luck' – For
    example, no matter what happens, good
    or bad, you chalk it up to luck. When it
    comes to luck, you need to stop and take a
    look at the things that you have
    accomplished in your life, how your own
    talents and smarts played a large role in
    successes that you have had, and look at
    how your personality played a role in
    these successful endeavors. Chances are
    that you have heard people say "You make
    your own luck." Remember this and live
    by it. It will help you start to see the
    successes that you make, and attribute
    them to your self-schema, not luck.

9. You purchase things that you do not like
    simply because you want to please other

people – For example, you buy a new house in a neighborhood that you do not care for and that you cannot afford simply to please your parents, spouse, or friends. Purchasing items that you really do not like only to please others sounds ridiculous, does it not? Reading it in print, in front of your face, it should be easy to see where you have been doing this in your life just to please other people. To stop this, you will have to put your self-control in place and ask yourself seriously if you need that item before you purchase it.

10. You can never decide where to eat – For example, you are at lunch with a group of coworkers and they ask where you would

like to go but you just say you do not know, even if you really want to go to your favorite place. People that have negative self-schemas feel that if they speak their minds or make a decision, they are going to hurt someone's feelings. If they do make a decision, they immediately change their mind to try and please someone else they are with.

11. You live on your phone, no matter where you are – For example, when the conversation at the table slows down or stops, do you immediately pull out your phone instead of starting up another topic? People who have negative self-schemas tend to live in their phones. Instead of starting up the conversation

again, speaking to someone new at a party, or mingling with people they already know, they will immediately pull their phone out and try to hide in something familiar. If you find that you do this, make yourself leave your phone in your purse or pocket and study things around the room if you do not know anyone else and are not comfortable starting the next topic.

12. You invite people that you do not like to parties and events – For example, there is one coworker or other student that you cannot stand, however you invite them to every party because you are worried about either keeping the peace and not making someone mad or that person is considered

popular and you have to have them like you. If you realize that you are inviting someone that you do not like to everything, it is time to stop. You have to realize, and tell yourself, that bad events in your life (such as someone not liking you) are not life-ending problems. Just because you do not invite someone to an event or party, you will not lose all of your other friends or be a social pariah. There is no reason to invite someone that is going to make you miserable to your event.

13. You hide in your room, your house, your office, etc – For example, if your coworker is angry at you for some reason, you tend to hide in your office, find reasons to be

off of your normal floor, or even call in sick. No one really loves confrontation. However, if you find that you hide from others so that you do not have to voice your own feelings about an issue, then negative self-schema has taken over. If you realize that you are doing this now, make sure that you are putting positive affirmations in your daily routine to help you reprogram those negative imprints.

14. You take constructive criticism too seriously – For example, when someone points out that a specific font you used on a paper is a bit small for them to read, you break down crying as soon as you are out of the room. This is another issue that many people suffer from. Any type of

constructive criticism completely catches you off guard and causes you serious emotional upset and it embarrasses you. One way that you can start to combat this is to count to 4 before you respond.

15. You cannot handle a compliment – For example, your friend says she loves your new blouse and you find fifty reasons why it is terrible. On the other side of not being able to take constructive criticism is not being able to take a compliment. If you find that even a simple compliment about how nice you smell or the like can pull several negative responses from you immediately, then you need to work on positive views of your opinions and your 'self'.

16. You constantly compare yourself with everyone else – For example, you publish a book and all you can think about is how Steven King has published way more than you. When you compare yourself to other people that you see as being more successful than you, you immediately take a huge hit to your own self-schema. Instead of worrying about what you have not done, go over what you have accomplished and overcome to get where you are now.

17. You hit the road as soon as sex is over – For example, you have been dating an amazing person for over a year, but every time you have sex, you immediately feel that you have to leave. The overwhelming

urge to leave right after sex with someone that you have been intimate with for a period of time is a characteristic of a negative self-schema. You are probably worried that they will not accept you for some reason, even if you have been dating for a while. People who have a hard working negative self-schema tend to have problematic relationships because they feel that they are not worthy of someone else's attention or love.

18. You have one odd, gross habit that you already know you do when you are nervous, upset, etc – For example, you are always picking at the skin around your fingernails to the point you have scabs and sores constantly. Everyone has gross

habits, but some cross the line into compulsive self-mutilation. Self-mutilation comes in many forms (nail biting, skin picking, pulling out your hair, or even cutting yourself) and is a key sign for those with negative self-schemas. Chances are when you read that sign and noticed that you do this, you already call it a nervous habit. To change this, it will take willpower and a strong push to stop. You can start with something as small as buying a fidget spinner or cube, writing your feelings down in a journal, or finding a hobby that you can get engrossed in. However, some types of self-mutilation (such as cutting yourself), are more

serious and need professional help to
stop.

19. You take naps, a lot – For example, you do
not have a health issue that causes fatigue
and you catch yourself sleeping all
weekend and missing social events. There
is a wide range of health issues that cause
fatigue, however a negative self-schema
that is working overtime can wear you
down. Your 'self' is using these long and
frequent naps to avoid social events, when
you have too much on your to do list, or
when you have fallen into the realm of
depression. If you are worried that you
might have depression, talk to your doctor
for advice or contact a psychologist who

can help you work through the issues at the root of the problem.

There are several other signs that you can look for in yourself to see if you have problems with a negative self-schema. Some of these include:

1. Not taking photographs of yourself or allowing others to do so

2. Always talking about yourself or your body in a negative tone

3. Never shopping for clothing for yourself

4. Being obsessed with how much you weigh

5. Putting off doing things you want to do because you feel that you need to lose weight first

6. Never looking in the mirror or liking anything you see in the mirror

7. Overthinking people's actions or comments to you, even when they are positive

8. Being overly defensive about everything

9. Continually putting other people down

10. Unable to be assertive in any situation

11. Lacking self-confidence about things that you are very good at

12. Obsessive behaviors

13. Problems with personal boundaries and personal space

14. Poor relationship skills

15. Poor social skills

16. Trying to float through life without effort or conflict

17. Being a workaholic

18. Having unreasonable expectations of
other people, events, ideas, etc.

So, what do you do if you find that you have any of these negative self-schemas? By recognizing that you have them, you have taken the first step to fixing them and replacing them with positive ones.

Starting Down The Right Path

All too often, our negative self-schemas come from comments that have been made by other people, as we discussed at the beginning of this chapter. When we allow these to sink in, even if they were never meant as negative information, it begins to taint our 'self'. Then, it begins to feel like we are actually criticizing ourselves when we have just taken other people's comments as truth. It sinks in to such a deep level in our 'self' that we no longer know the difference.

To begin seeing yourself in a positive light, you have to start changing the negativity in your 'self'. Now, this will not happen overnight and it will mean hard work on your part. However, by starting down the road of positivity, you will find that it gets easier as you start peeling away the negative layers and rebuilding with positive reinforcements.

Starting To Gain Control Of The Negative

Now that you know several of the most common signs of a negative self-schema's impact, you can begin to gain control again. There are many people out there who think that they cannot make any impact on their negative self-images on their own. They do not believe that they can ever change the cycle that they are on, so they never try. The fact that you are reading this shows you are not one of those people. You have the ability to change your negative self-schemas into positive ones.

First, you need to know that feelings are far more powerful than thoughts. Emotions are the tools that you used to build up this negative foundation and images, and those feelings are also what help keep us shielded from bad things in our lives. The good news is that you can start to change these feelings and emotions by beginning with your thoughts. Just remember that you have to work at this, you have to consciously try to change these negative self-schemas. The negative images did not get there overnight and they are not going to go away that fast either.

Here are several ways to start gaining control of your emotions and the negative feelings that you have been allowing to control your 'self' view:

Be Calm, Be Objective, Be Positive

The key to this step is to learn to see yourself from outside, being calm and objective. This allows you to bypass the distortion that fear, narcissism, pride, and all those other negative emotions so that you only view yourself through a calm, objective assessment. You do not have to believe that you are as beautiful as your favorite actress, as thin as the latest batch of runway models, or as rich as Bill Gates. However, you do have to objectively realize that every person is different.

Once you start with that fact, you then move on to focusing on what you have learned throughout your life. These lessons are those that associate with your strengths, not downfalls. Focus on the things that you have learned throughout your life so far that have made you a better person.

Now, consider if your younger self was a whole other person, and you were teaching that child about the lessons that you have learned. Only focus on these strengths, and help your younger self work through problems that you faced then. For example, if you know now that you are an excellent artist, yet kids made fun of you for always drawing in school, you can help your younger self realize that it was a natural talent and nothing to be ashamed of.

As you work through these lessons, you will find that there is negative information that has imprinted itself on your 'self' view. You may not wipe it all away this first time, but you will make a dent in how these negative views affect your self-schema. Remember that you were conditioned to that negative view, and you have to remove it over time as you peel through the layers. In fact, you may never completely wipe away the negative layers. However, you can learn to see yourself objectively and begin to place positive layers over that 'self' to eventually crush the negative.

Stop Comparing

The next step that you need to take on the path to a positive self-schema is to stop comparing yourself to others. We are all born into this world the same. We only have our own awareness and a blank canvas where we have not developed a 'self' yet. As you now know, our 'self' is created as we grow and there will always be negative aspects that rear their heads. One of the main ways that we gain negative self-schemas is by comparing ourselves to others.

From young ages, we are taught that we have to compare ourselves to everyone else. We are shown people on TV and told that they are 'beautiful' or 'handsome', so we begin to think we have to look like that to be happy. We are then shown people who are successful and wealthy and we begin to think we have to be like that to be successful. And then the list grows.

So, we unconsciously begin to compare ourselves to everyone else around us without even realizing that we are doing it. Once we start doing that, we always find places where we do not stack up to others and consider that a failure on our own part. We never stop to realize that we are not that person we are comparing ourselves to and we never will be. We forget that we are all individuals for a reason. Instead, we feel that we do not stack up to that other person and we cannot be perfect on that particular aspect. When we feel that we can never be perfect in some way, which is unrealistic to begin with, we begin to only think about the negative aspects of that thought.

Living your life through a constant comparison of other people, especially comparisons that you put yourself through, causes your self-schema to become bitter, paranoid, vain, and extremely damaged. You are constantly worrying about how you look, what you are wearing, how your hair is cut or colored, and what people think about you. This tainted view of yourself will also taint that wonder that you had as a child, when you could easily be spontaneous since you had not placed this negative view on your 'self'.

Usually, when someone is in the cycle of comparing themselves to others for a long period of time, they realize that they are doing it. In fact, they will often tell themselves that they wish they were more like those people that do not care what others think – even though this is still comparing themselves to another person. They understand that they have to learn to think about themselves differently. However, it is a hard habit to change that requires a conscious effort on their part to stop the constant comparisons.

By recognizing the different negative aspects that comparing yourself to others does, it will cause you to stop and think about those constant comparisons. As those thoughts seep into your head, you can begin to combat them and banish them from your mind. It will take work and a constant effort to ensure that you replace those negative thoughts with positive ones about yourself. However, the more you do it, the easier it will become and the bigger the change you will see in your self-schema.

Saying No Is Ok Too

Many of us have a hard time saying 'no' when we are asked to help out with something. We often feel that we cannot say no because we are taught to fear authority, to not hurt people's feelings, and not let people down. So, we end up saying yes to things that we cannot possibly finish or even fit into our schedule. If we do start or possibly finish the project, usually the work is half-hearted and it is obvious that we just rushed through it.

Not only can other people tell that it was rushed or half-hearted, but you know it also. Then, you are unhappy with yourself that you did not do the job like you felt it needed to be done. Once that sets in, you feel the need to do more projects for people to make up for it. You then take on more tasks that you do not have time for or cannot handle, and they end up being the same as the first one. It turns into a cycle that is hard to break.

Another problem with saying yes to everything is that people will expect you to help with everything. Once people know they can get you to say yes to chairing a committee, helping with things at your kid's school, and so on, they will ask for your help with other projects continually. Then, you will feel that you cannot say no because you have helped with so much that it's expected.

To break this cycle, it will take more self-control and a strong will to say no. You do not have to be rude about saying no or make up excuses. Instead, say what you mean and be firm with your decision. When you can say no without being rude, and say it with a firm manner, it will become easier for you to make solid decisions about other aspects of your life and it will boost your self-esteem. Boosting your self-esteem by being able to be firm with your decisions will help chip away at the negative self-schemas that have built up.

Quit Pretending To Be Something You Are Not

We have all been guilty of trying to pretend to be something or someone we are not simply to impress or please someone else. It does not matter if this was on a first date or the first day of school, eventually you had to come clean about who you are. The reason that we do this is because we are scared to be our authentic selves because we are scared that people will not like us.

Unfortunately, you cannot please everyone all the time and you cannot fool everyone all of the time. You have to understand that there will be people that you come into contact with throughout your life who may not like you. The fear of that realization may almost paralyze some people, but it is a fact that everyone has to face. It is not the end of the world however.

Once you understand that you should be your authentic self, you will find that it is extremely liberating. With that liberty, you will be able to boost your view of your 'self' and see that you are a unique and awesome person, just as you are. When you are yourself without any false stories or pretending to be someone you are not, you will be a much happier person.

Realize That You Can Make Mistakes

We are taught from a young age that mistakes are a horrible thing. However, if we do not make mistakes, we cannot learn. No one likes to fail, but it is a part of life. When you understand that you can allow yourself to fail, and promise to learn from those mistakes, you will realize the importance of your mistakes.

When you understand that everyone else in the world makes mistakes, even people who may seem perfect in your eyes, the world becomes a much softer place. It also allows your 'self' to see that you do not have to be perfect or pretend to be. Knowing that mistakes are a natural part of being human will help chip away at that negative image that has built up in your mind and help you relax.

Taking Responsibility

As mentioned above, we all hate to admit that we make mistakes. So, when they happen, our first instinct is to try and cover them up or shift the blame. There are some people who have managed to overcome this fear and they are able to take responsibility for their own mistakes and actions. Now, not all actions that you take are going to wind up being mistakes. However, you have to learn to take responsibility for things that you do, good or bad, in order to start removing the negative self-schema that has built up around your decision making process.

To take responsibility for your actions, you need to start learning to say that you are sorry when you make a mistake, hurt someone's feelings, break something, etc. Saying that we are sorry for something is really difficult for some people, so this can be an extremely tough step to take. Practice makes perfect, so you can go over what you need to say to apologize before you have to confront a mistake that you have made. If you need to, practice in front of a mirror so that you can hear the words out loud.

When you do apologize for something that you have done, follow that up by asking how you can help to fix something. This will show a genuine effort on your part to fixing things so everyone is happy. The key to this part is that you have to follow up on what you said that you were going to do. It will take effort on your part, however, it will go a long way in helping you reverse the negative emotions that go along with making a mistake or hurting someone else.

Take Time To Help Other People

It does not matter what your status is, how much money you make, or what you look like, you can always find ways to help other people. Helping by volunteering your time, donating items, or just doing someone for someone else will take you away from the things in your own life that you are overstressing about. You suddenly are no longer wrapped up in your own problems and you start seeing the bigger picture in life, that you are not the only one with problems out there. You will see that your role in the universe is more than you realize and that you can make a difference in someone else's life.

Do not worry about who sees you donate items, who watches you volunteer your time. You do not need to help other people to further yourself in life. Instead, give freely, help anywhere that you can, and do anything that you can do. For some people, simply having someone to talk to can be a tremendous help in their life and offer them a little bit of hope that they need to make it through.

Focus On Something And Go For It

Focus is something that many of us lose at different times in our lives. The key is to stop worrying about what choice you made by second-guessing everything that you do. Take responsibility for what you want to do. For example, if you want to do yoga but have never done it, learn how to commit to doing it. If you want to make loose-leaf tea at home, learn how to make it, gather the items and ingredients, then do it.

You cannot worry about how the tea will come out or how you might look learning yoga. Do not give a second thought to the idea that someone else may not like what you are doing. If you let that worry set in, you will never learn yoga, you will never learn to make loose-leaf tea, and so on.

Worry can be a paralyzing fear that stops us from doing things that we want to do.

Instead, take a deep breath and just dive in. Learn about what you want to do, do it, and move on if you do not like it. Do not learn new things for others, make sure that you are doing these things for yourself. Learning new things, doing things that scare you, and figuring out how to dodge that worry of what someone else might think is a huge step towards building positive self-schemas.

Chapter Seven: Making Positive Changes To Your Self-Schema

So, you have a firm understanding of what self-schemas are, how they are made, what they can do, the negative schemas that drag down our 'self' view, and how to start on the road to replacing negativity with positive changes. Now, it is time to fully get on the path to making positive changes to your self-schemas that will become a permanent part of your 'self'.

As you go through implementing these positive changes in your self-schema and reprogramming the negative aspects, keep in mind that none of this will be an overnight fix. One of the main reasons that we went so in-depth with what the self-schema is, how it is created, and all of the aspects that go into the multiplicity of them throughout your life, is to show how long this 'self' programming has been put in place. It took a long time for all of these schemas to incorporate themselves into your psyche. It will not be something that can be fixed by flipping a switch. You will need to work at these things, practice, and ensure that you do as much as you can each day to work on them.

You will start to see changes in how you view the world and people around you as you begin down this path of creating positive self-schemas. When you realize that you understand why some things are negative, how a coworker's comment affected you and how you refused to let it sink in, and so on, you are truly on the right path to creating those positive self-schemas that you want.

So, let's get into the different tools that you can use to banish those negative views and replace them with positive ones.

Experience Everything In That Moment

Focus on the moment at hand and not what you need to do at home tonight or what you are doing this weekend. Choose your own actions wisely and make conscious efforts to do positive things. Do not allow the negativity of the past to creep in and taint the new things that you are putting into place. If you allow negativity to creep in and you realize it is there, stop and close your eyes for a moment and push them out of your mind with a couple of deep breaths. Live for that moment that you are in now. Enjoy it and realize there will never be another one like it.

Learn To Be Aware

Now that you have learned how negative images form in our minds, you are aware of two different things. The first is that you can see when comments, images, or other negative information is being thrown your way and block it. The second is that you can see where your own actions, comments, or other information that you are putting out to someone else can be hurtful. Make an effort to always be aware of how you process information and purposefully discard negative information. Also, make an effort to be aware of how your comments, views, and information can make a negative impact on someone around you.

Do Not Judge Anyone – Even Yourself

While this is a hard one to overcome because you have been programmed to do it, you have to take steps to stop judging other people and yourself. Accept others around you for who they are and love them for it. Accept yourself for who you are and love yourself for it. Accept mistakes and successes and move towards only positive attitudes and information about them all.

Keep Yourself Connected

When you are mindful of yourself, you will develop a sense of connection to your 'self' and all of the positive and negative aspects. This connection will help you reduce the urge to please others by taking your self-schema off of auto pilot when it comes to allowing the opinions of others to rule your choices in life. As you strengthen this connection every day, you will eventually find that your negative self-schema that required you to please everyone around you has faded and a positive one has replaced it.

Mindful Meditation

You may not be someone who meditates, however it is a technique that you need to learn. Mindful meditation means that you stop, focus on your breathing, and let go of all those thoughts that are racing through your mind. Accept that those racing thoughts, beliefs, and feelings that you have always had cluttered up there are simply transient things – not permanent parts of yourself. You do not have to meditate for hours, just a few minutes each day. That time will help you focus on only your breathing and clearing the cluttering negativity from your mind.

Actively Participate

All too often we stop participating in our own lives. When you begin to practice mindful meditation every day, you will find the encouragement to take an active part in your own life once more. Being mindful of yourself will help you become active in creating a positive role in your life. It will help you choose your responses to thoughts and emotions and discard the negative ones in lieu of the positive ones.

Let Your Inner Child's Mind Through

We mentioned a few times throughout this book that no one is born with this negativity ingrained in them. You need to learn to let your inner child's mind come through and see things in a new light. Learn to view the world like you are seeing it for the first time. By intentionally seeing things as something brand new, you will see where you have held negative images of too many things for too long. When you come across those new things, boot them out of your mind and take in new, positive views.

Be Able To Let Go

Another perk that comes with being mindful is learning to let go. Non-attachment means that you are able to let go of previously held 'truths' that required you to be someone you are not. Letting go allows you to choose who you are and trust in your own view of your 'self' as the best one of all.

Show Yourself Compassion

Realize that you deserve as much compassion, love, and friendship as anyone else in the world.

By having self-compassion, you are able to see the value in your 'self' and your positive self-schemas and allow them to help you make better, positive choices. This new view of your 'self' will also help steer you away from dangerous relationships, negative situations, and other aspects of your life that have been causing the negative self-schemas to run the show for too long.

Keep A Journal

One physical aspect of your journey should be a journal. Write down your feelings and thoughts that feel trapped in your subconscious. Letting them flow through a pen, pencil, or even your keyboard will help you get a release from their hold on you. It will also help you separate the

positive from the negative and see where you

have been holding onto too many negative

aspects of your self-schemas.

Chapter Eight: Creating The Self-Schema You Want

As you have read through the previous chapters, you have come across some aspects of yourself that you realize are extremely negative. Some may have already been known to you, but some may have been a complete surprise. These surprise negative self-schemas probably have had you thinking throughout the remainder of this book, wondering if that specific aspect of your self-schema has caused problems in jobs, relationships, and other aspects of your life.

Now comes the time when you learn how to create the self-schemas that you want. You learn to replace the negative ones with positive ones and truly become the person that you want to be.

Congratulations for undertaking this journey and realizing that the negativity that has been cluttering up your 'self' needs to be removed and replaced with something better.

Positive Self-Schemas Are Emotional Not Self-Image Driven

Building new positive self-schemas that will overcome the negative ones mean that you need to change how you feel about yourself as a person on an emotional level. We have already gone through the different problems that negative body self-schemas create and how they can cause physical and health problems. Now, you have to learn to push out the negative self-schema that you are not good enough. It does not matter what you think you are not good enough in, such as looks, size, talent, etc. What matters is that you push that thought out and replace it with the fact that you are good enough when you are your true self. Replace that negative thought with the positive one on a daily basis until it becomes the auto-drive that controls the positive self-schema that you want.

Remove Unrealistic Views Of Perfection

You have a set view of what perfection and success looks like that has been ingrained as you have grown up. It may change at times, but it has always stayed on a similar path. You need to take a hard look at these views and focus on whether each one is a positive or negative view. If you have this view because it was imprinted on you to make a parent, other family member, or friend happy, then it is a negative view. If it is there because you feel that you have to impress other people, it is a negative view.

Views of perfection and success need to make you feel happy inside. They need to evoke positive emotions inside your psyche that make you want to reach those goals for you, not for anyone else. If you find that your views revolve around negative self-schemas, you want to take a hard look at them and discard ones that do not give you a happy emotion from them. Instead, consider what would truly make you happy inside, what would make the real you consider yourself a success. Those are the positive self-schemas that you want to have about your views of perfection and success.

While the idea of dissolving your image of perfection and success seems a bit counter-productive, keep in mind that you are taking the negative self-schema that you have built up and replacing it with the positive one that you want. If you take a hard look at the perceptions you have now of those two aspects and you find that they do make you truly happy inside, then keep them.

Replace Self-Rejection With Confidence

As we discussed in previous chapters, you have already begun to see where you have been programmed to automatically reject yourself from certain situations, relationships, etc. This form of self-rejection is a huge negative self-schema that you have learned to use as a defense mechanism over the years. By seeing how you may be using defense mechanisms to protect yourself from hurt and rejection, you should already have identified several areas where you do this automatically. Now that you know you do this automatically, you have taken the first step to removing this automatic self-rejection.

Start focusing on this self-rejection as it happens, force yourself to stop and take a breath. Push the negativity out as you breathe out, and you may have to take a couple of breaths before you feel that it is gone enough to move on. Once it is gone, you can begin to replace those negative thoughts with positive ones. While they might sound silly, they will do wonders to push a positive self-schema into the void the negative one is leaving. You need to remind yourself that you are good enough, you do deserve this, and you do not care what others will think. Keep reminding yourself of these things and focus them on the event or idea. Remind yourself that you can do this, you understand what has to happen to make it successful, and you will knock it out of the ballpark.

Change Your Beliefs To Change Your Emotions

When your beliefs are firmly planted, they will control how you feel emotionally about a subject. If you believe that you are not good enough, then you will allow your emotions to rule how you deal with everything. This is because these negative beliefs give birth to emotions of fear and insecurity. For example, if you believe that you do not deserve that promotion, emotionally you will sabotage any chance you have of getting that promotion – or may not even ask for it at all.

Our belief system is put into place as our self-schemas develop throughout our lives. They become so deep that they control everything else around them. If you have a positive self-schema about being good enough, then the emotions that surround decisions about successes will push you toward great outcomes. However, if you have a negative self-schema about never being good enough for anything, the emotional toll that it will take is a hefty one.

You have already taken the main step: determining if you have a negative self-schema that you want to change. The next step is to understand that you, and only you, are the one who is observing your personal 'self' image. We are not the self-image itself, we are only the viewer – and the most important viewer of all. You have to realize that there is no one else whose views of your 'self' are more important. If you are happy with you, others around you will be as well. However, if you are not happy, everyone will realize that too. Possessing this awareness will help you shift the focus and take the next step in creating a positive self-schema to replace the negative belief.

You must now start on the path to putting a positive belief system in place. Focus on aspects

of your life that you already consider positive –
no matter what they are. Go over your beliefs
about those positive areas and see where they
stem from. Next, start to focus on the negative
aspects, where you have the belief that you are
not good enough for that particular job, to date a
certain person, live in a specific neighborhood,
etc. Begin to copy over those positive beliefs and
transform them to fit the hole that the negative
beliefs have left.

You will have to practice this every day. Some
days will be hard and you will have to continually
repeat these new, positive self-schemas all day.
Other days, it will seem that they have already
switched to the positive beliefs. It will not take
long and you will wake up one day to realize that
the positive self-schema is on auto pilot and

controlling your emotional state in a positive way.

You Are Not Just An Image, You Are The Creator

The last step in putting positive self-schemas in place is to realize that you are not just an image in your mind. You are not just an image in anyone's mind. Instead, you are the creator of this image. You create all aspects of your image, good and bad. You have the power to remove the negative self-schemas that you have now identified and banish them from your image forever. You also have the power to put forth positive self-schemas in their place.

Realizing this is the first part of this step.

Practicing placing positive images that you control is a step that you must do every day.

Conclusion

You should now have a firm grip on which self-schemas you have in place are negative and which are positive. You also have a solid framework to help you change the negative ones into those that you want to possess. The rest of the process is all up to you. The more that you practice these steps, the faster they will become a part of your 'self' and set on autopilot.

As you continue on your journey toward overcoming your negative self-schemas, you will have moments where you realize that you have changed. You will find that you no longer invite people you do not like to events and parties. You will find that you no longer are worried if your mother is happy with the car you drive or the neighborhood you live in. You will find that you truly have removed negative self-schemas and have a strong, positive one in place.

The best part is that you will also start to see changes happen in your life that you know are not just luck. They will be changes that you have created.